The Special Stories Series

Joe's Special Story

by **KATE GAYNOR**

illustrated by **AILEEN MURPHY**

Published in 2008 by

SPECIAL STORIES PUBLISHING

Member of CLÉ – The Irish Book Publishers Association

ISBN 978-0-9555787-1-7

A catalogue record for this book is available from the British Library

Printed by

BELVEDERE PRINT LTD. DUBLIN, IRELAND

Special Stories Publishing

www.specialstories.net

Acknowledgements

Many thanks to Kieran, my father Michael, my brother George and my extended family and friends, my uncle Liam Gaynor, Liz O'Donoghue, Eva Byrne and the Louth County Enterprise Board for their endless encouragement, support and invaluable advice.

A special thanks to social worker Grainne O'Malley from The Adoption Authority of Ireland and also to Bronagh McKenna, H.S.E. Foster Care Services Team, Dundalk, Co. Louth.

Special thanks also to Dr. Gerard Molloy Ph.D C.Psychol. whose time and effort with this project was so greatly appreciated.

About the Illustrator

Aileen Murphy is an artist who lives in Dublin. She grew up in the country side of Co. Wicklow and studied in the The National College of Art and Design. She now works in her studio in Dublin City drawing and making various 3D art. Aileen's artwork usually relates to Fairy tales, girlhood motifs and wacky dreams. In the future she wants to travel to Iceland, illustrate many more children's books, have many art exhibitions and eventually move closer to the country side so she can own a dog and a vegetable garden.

To read more about the special stories collection, visit the Special Stories website at:
www.specialstories.net

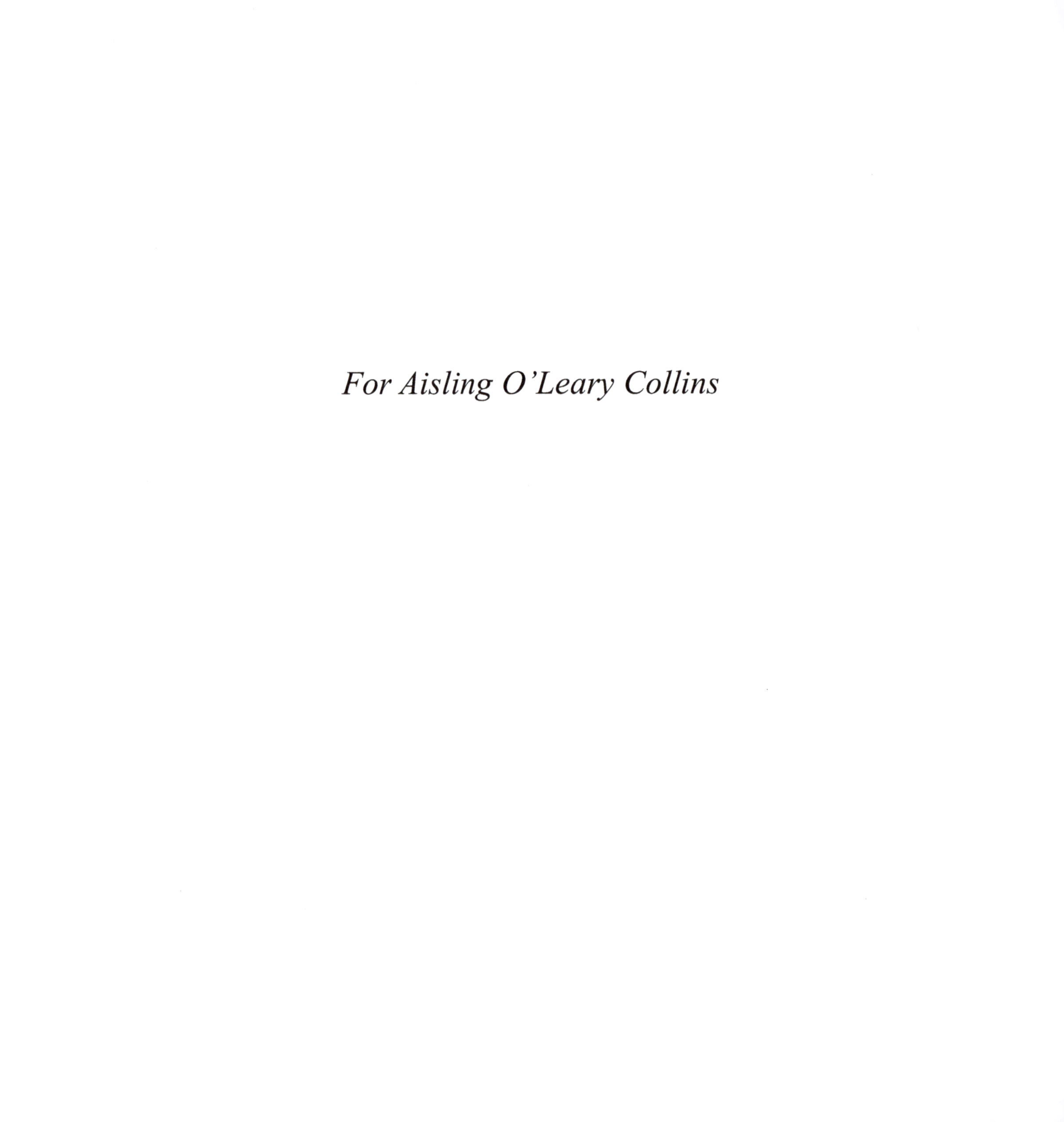

For Aisling O'Leary Collins

Hi! my name is **Joe**. I am five years old.

I live with my Mum, Dad and older brother George in a big blue house near the sea. But I didn't always live with the Mum, Dad and big brother that I do now.

A lot of children grow up and live with the same mums and dads their whole lives and they are called a family.

But other children, like me, live with a different mum or dad than the ones they had when they were born and they are called a family too.

Even though we all have a birth mum and dad, not everyone can stay with their birth mum and dad for their whole lives. There are lots of reasons why this happens and everyone's story is different.

But when it does happen, a mum and dad from another family can become your new mum and dad instead.

When you become part of a new family and have a different mum and dad to the ones you had when you were born it is sometimes called adoption.

My mum says that adoption stories are very special. Sometimes she tells me the story about when I was adopted, which I like a lot.

The story always starts with the long journey that she and my dad had to take to bring me home when I was only a small baby.

My dad says that everyone, even Bonnie the big black and white dog, was so happy when I finally arrived.

They couldn't wait to have a little boy just like me to come and live with them and become part of their family forever and ever.

Sometimes I think about the country where I was born and about my birth mum and dad. Sometimes I feel sad that I can't see them.

When I feel like this, my mum and I take out the very special book that my mum and dad made for me. It is called 'Joe's Special Story Book'.

It has pictures and stories about the country that I came from and where I was born. My mum says that it's ok to feel sad sometimes and to think about your birth mum and dad.

She says that talking to someone always helps you to feel better.
My Dad says that some day when I'm older, I might learn more
about my country and about my birth mum or dad.

In my big blue house near the sea I have my very own room with my own bed and my own little window looking out at the waves.

That's where I keep my special book about the country that I came from and how we all became a family.

After looking at the book I sometimes go for a swim with my mum. My dog Bonnie loves splashing around and trying to catch the fish with her big fat paws!

18

When I see my dad and my big brother George waving at me from the sand I remember just how special my story and my family really are.

So what about you? Do you have a special story like mine?
Why don't you tell me all about it on your Special Story Page?

Your Special Story Page

SPECIAL
STORIES

Notes for Grown Ups on Adoption

Adoption is a legal procedure which permanently places a child with a person who is not that child's biological mother or father. The adopted child is then entitled to all privileges belonging to a natural child of the adoptive parents.

Adoption law and practice varies greatly from country to country however there are two main types of adoption as regards location of the child.

Domestic Adoption: This is the placement of a child within the country in which he or she was born and lives.

Intercountry/International Adoption: This is the placement of a child outside that child's country of birth.

Intra-family adoption: This is when the child is adopted by a close member of their family e.g. step-parent adoption.

Foster parent adoption: When the child is adopted by his or her foster parents.

Open adoption: When the birth and adoptive parents have some contact up to and/or after the adoption becomes legal.

Closed adoption: When the birth and adoptive parents share no information or contact whatsoever. This can be simply a personal choice or as a result of a court order.

How to use this book

Any child who has been through the adoption process will naturally have questions about the story behind their adoption. For children who have been adopted through inter-country adoption this is sometimes even more prevalent. This book has been designed for parents, teachers and social workers to read with children who have been adopted from a different country to the one they live in now. By reading the story with your child and discussing the experience of a child in a similar situation, you can take the opportunity to discuss any feelings of unhappiness or doubt that the child might have as regards his/her own situation.

For information on adoption please contact your local government agency or association.

Other books from Special Stories Publishing

A FAMILY FOR SAMMY: This story was written to help explain the foster care process to young children.

FIRST PLACE: This story aims to help children to understand and accept the effects of cleft palate, cleft lip or any speech impediment in their lives and most importantly, how best to overcome them.

THE WINNER: The intention of this book is to help explain Asthma and its effects to young children.

THE BRAVEST GIRL IN SCHOOL: The objective of this story is to help children with diabetes to appreciate the importance of taking their insulin injections and being aware of what they eat.

THE FAMOUS HAT: The goal of this book is to help children with leukaemia (or other forms of cancer) to prepare for treatment, namely chemotherapy, and a stay in hospital.

THE LOST PUPPY: This book has been designed to help children with limited mobility to see the positive aspects that using a wheelchair can bring to their lives.

To read more about the special stories collection, visit the Special Stories website at:
www.specialstories.net

www.ingramcontent.com/pod-product-compliance
Lightning Source LLC
Chambersburg PA
CBHW040905070726
47599CB00038B/2306